Not by Bread Alone

Daily Reflections for Lent 2017

P9-CEO-913

Genevieve Glen

LITURGICAL PRESS

Collegeville, Minnesota

www.litpress.org

Nihil Obstat: Reverend Robert Harren, *Censor deputatus*

Imprimatur: ✠ Most Reverend Donald J. Kettler, J.C.L.,
Bishop of Saint Cloud, Minnesota, May 17, 2016.

Cover design by Monica Bokinskie. Photo courtesy of Thinkstock.

ISSN: 1552-8782

ISBN: 978-0-8146-4710-3   978-0-8146-4735-6 (ebook)

Introduction

Lent is the desert season. That cliché means something different to me now after living in the desert for several years. The Arizona desert is not the Sahara. Creosote scrub surrounded us, punctuated by graceful palo verde fronds and the tall thorny poles of saguaro. Roadrunners and quail sped across the unpaved roads in front of the car. Coyotes broke the night quiet, terrorizing the jackrabbits, prairie dogs, and other small furry creatures that abounded. And, yes, there were rattlesnakes.

The snakes were the ones who set me to wondering: Where does the desert population find its water? Seasonal rains don't account for it. Streambeds are mostly dry. Any pools are artificial and chlorinated. Water lies beneath the desert floor, but human beings have to dig wells to reach it. And there lies the answer: roots. Desert plants dig down deep to drink. Furred animals and reptiles know how to search out the threads of water signaled by green growth or how to drink from succulents. But desert water is mostly hidden from the casual human eye.

Lent is the desert season, when we go out into the harsh places of the spirit to find the living water believers will celebrate at Easter. The readings challenge us to look to the roots of our own attitudes, words, and actions. They offer us tools: maps of the paths to life we may have strayed from and painful warnings about the poisoned wells we might be tempted to drink from. They unmask the tricks of the

Tempter who clouds our direction with mirages. And, over and over again, they show us the ever-present Christ from whom the living waters flow and in whom alone we will find our way. Otherwise the bad news we might read about ourselves at the roots of a parched life honestly examined could blind us to the good news of God's love, which never runs dry.

The desert is not poetry. It is a reality that makes heavy demands on those who would cross it. We're asked to abandon the padded comforts we use to protect ourselves from the vulnerability of love and the hard work it requires. We're asked to let the desert sun, the Light of the World, shine in all the heart's corners we would rather not see. We risk losing the shelter of our carefully built tents to the great Wind that whips across the desert sands and through the Upper Room at Pentecost. We're asked for humility, truthfulness, and perseverance through faith's dark desert nights. But when we raise our eyes from our own discomfort, we see the flame of the distant paschal candle and know that we do not travel alone.

Welcome to the adventure!

Reflections

March 1: Ash Wednesday

Heart Work

Readings: Joel 2:12-18; 2 Cor 5:20–6:2; Matt 6:1-6, 16-18

Scripture:
Rend your hearts, not your garments . . . (Joel 2:13)

Reflection: Why? Tearing clothing and wearing ashes were traditional biblical signs of mourning and repentance. But rending hearts?

Odd as this exhortation sounds, it pinpoints Lent's starting point: the heart. In the biblical world, the heart was seen as the inner workshop where thought and feeling come together to forge experience into wisdom. Wisdom hammers out our worldview and our values. From them we make our daily choices and decisions. What we do starts in the heart (see Matt 15:18-20).

So Lent is first of all heart work. Like cooks, carpenters, artists, and householders, we are invited to turn out the cupboards and closets of the heart to see what's stored there. Are some of our habits of thinking and doing getting stale? Are some of them troublemakers? Are some of them bogging down our spiritual journey with useless baggage? What needs to change? What needs to go?

We are also invited to take a look at God's past promptings now stuffed into the back of our spiritual cubbyholes and forgotten. What blessings has God left behind in previous

Lents and in the seasons in between (Joel 2:14)? What tools old *and* new do we already have that would help us with this year's heart work?

Lent is work, but we do not work alone. Before we cook up our own plans, some perhaps self-serving, the gospel acclamation directs us to begin with the kind of prayer that seeks to learn: "If today you hear [God's] voice, / harden not your hearts" (verse before the gospel; see Ps 95:8).

Lent is heart work. Jesus cautions us in today's gospel against confusing external changes—extra prayer for public show, alms trumpeted over coffee after Mass, piously gloomy faces pinched with fasting—with the changes that matter. Those are heart changes for the sake of life changes so that we can honestly make or renew our Easter baptismal commitment to live in Christ.

Rend your hearts, not your garments.

Meditation: What changes is God calling you to make this Lent "in my thoughts and in my words, / in what I have done and in what I have failed to do" as we pray at Mass? What heart changes will they require?

Prayer: God of mercy and compassion, grant that we may undertake our Lenten heart work with honesty, courage, and humility so that it may become for us a healing remedy (see prayer after Communion).

March 2: Thursday after Ash Wednesday

The Burden Borne

Readings: Deut 30:15-20; Luke 9:22-25

Scripture:
"If anyone wishes to come after me, he must deny
    himself
and take up his cross daily and follow me." (Luke 9:23)

Reflection: Moses says, "Choose life" (Deut 30:19)! Who wouldn't? The Holocaust of World War II and the genocides in our day have produced incredible stories from people like Walter Ciszek, SJ, and Immaculée Ilibagiza of choosing to live, even amid impossible horror. Yet Jesus tells us that we must choose more than just breathing in and out. True life carries a high price: "Take up your cross," not once but every day, and "follow me."

Long repetition has narrowed the meaning of this familiar exhortation down to bearing life's sufferings, and perhaps even adding to them voluntarily. Certainly patient endurance under pains great and small is an essential dimension of Jesus' cross, but it is only a slice of the larger reality of Jesus' life. He carried that bar of rough wood on shoulders already torn and bleeding only in the last hours of his life. But he bore the reason for it all his life: unyielding love for every human being, even his enemies.

That burden surely wore him down: he spent hours under a hot sun teaching, healing, and casting out demons. Every time, he could have said that power went out from him (cf. Mark 5:25-34). But he never took a day off. Exhausted and resting by a Samaritan well, he took on a sinner in need (John 4:4-42). Perhaps hungry himself after hours of preaching and curing the sick, he multiplied bread for the throng instead of going for lunch (Matt 14:13-21). Thirsty, he even refused drugged wine on the cross (Matt 27:34).

Love that takes responsibility for others was his lifelong burden—and he shouldered it gladly for the sake of the joy before him (Heb 12:2), the joy of knowing humanity was safe at last under the shadow of the cross.

Choose life? How? Take up the weight, light or heavy, of responsibility for others' good. Walter Ciszek knew that. Immaculée Ilibagiza knew that. Because they knew that survival without love is worthless. It costs the erosion of one's own soul. They learned it from Jesus.

Meditation: When does the burden of love chafe you? What most tempts you to lay down genuine responsibility for the sake of self-indulgence?

Prayer: Jesus, Cross-bearer, strengthen us to share in the love that chooses never to lay down its burden, no matter what the cost.

Wounded Eyesight

Readings: Isa 58:1-9a; Matt 9:14-15

Scripture:
Is this the manner of fasting I wish,
  of keeping a day of penance:
That a man bow his head like a reed
  and lie in sackcloth and ashes? . . .
This, rather, is the fasting that I wish:
  releasing those bound unjustly,
  untying the thongs of the yoke; . . .
Sharing your bread with the hungry,
  sheltering the oppressed and the homeless; . . .
Then . . . your wound shall quickly be healed . . .
  (Isa 58:6-8)

Reflection: Fasting, almsgiving, and prayer are the three pillars of Lent. Today Isaiah warns us against reading fasting through too small a lens. In an older Lenten tradition we fasted from certain amounts of food. Now we observe the Friday practice of fasting from meat.

My long-ago seventh-graders would ask, "Can you drink chicken bouillon from a mug since you're not eating it?" They wanted precise rules. It was a seventh-grade question: What exactly do I have to do? What can I get away with before God will get mad?

Such questions are symptoms of spiritual astigmatism in adults. Keeping an eye on how we look to God as we measure out parsimonious penances keeps our focus on ourselves: How am I doing?

God is much more interested in what we're doing than how we're doing. Penances like wearing sackcloth and ashes in biblical times or abstaining from meat today are not goals for us to be tested on. They are means to clear eyes clouded by looking so much at ourselves we can't look around and see others' suffering and need.

A touch of hunger opens the door into the streets of our world. A morsel of want lets us see more clearly there what Isaiah saw: human beings yoked and bound to others' material or emotional profits, made invisible by filthy clothing or others' disregard, destitute of resources or of purpose and of love. Tend to these wounds and others like them, says Isaiah, and your own will be healed.

Wounds? Yes, blinded eyes, hardened hearts, worries over our own standing before God that keep us from being what we are: brothers and sisters beloved by God and made one in Christ.

Meditation: Remember one unhappy face you've noticed. What caused it? Want, hunger, loneliness, fear? What is one thing you could do to lessen it? Start now!

Prayer: God of love, open our eyes to the suffering we never see around us; open our hearts to recognize our brothers and sisters in want; direct our steps toward help we could offer.

The Fasting Tongue

Readings: Isa 58:9b-14; Luke 5:27-32

Scripture:
If you remove from your midst oppression,
 false accusation and malicious speech . . .
"Repairer of the breach," they shall call you,
 "Restorer of ruined homesteads." (Isa 58:9b-12)

Reflection: Lenten penances sometimes appear to focus on what goes into our mouths, but Jesus himself said what comes out of them matters more (Matt 15:11). That's where the harm is done, to others and to ourselves. And that's what Isaiah calls us to fast from: false accusation and malicious speech.

Eavesdrop on some common conversations: "I heard that she had lunch with a married man on Wednesday," answered with "*I* heard it was her husband's best friend." Or, "You know, he's perfectly capable of making shady deals on the side. My next-door neighbor bragged about what he got out of it the last time." Or, "Have you seen the bruises on that kid's arm? They say he got them falling out of a tree. But *I* think . . ." Or just, "She looks awful in that dress. I'd say she's put on twenty pounds," or "His hair *must* be dyed."

The speaker may mean no real harm, but the words do damage nonetheless. Suspicions are planted, doubts sown, judgments insinuated, hints dropped. Many of them shade or distort or just plain falsify the truth Christians espouse when we are joined in baptism to the One who *is* the truth (John 14:6). All of them provoke cold shoulders turned, dislikes fueled, reputations muddied, relationships strained or severed. Hardly the work of love!

Fasting from damaging speech is a twofold job: we are called to fast from voicing falsehood or malice, but we are also called to refrain from listening to it. Such a fast might mean breaking off one's own harmful words in mid-sentence to say, "Sorry, that's an exaggeration," but it might also mean getting up from the table and saying, "Sorry, I just can't listen to this kind of gossip." Simple steps, but often not easy ones.

Nevertheless, the result may very well be what the prophet promises: broken relationships mended, ruined homesteads restored. Now *that* is the work of love Jesus is always busy about!

Meditation: Replay recent conversations. Which ones hurt speaker and hearer as well as those spoken about? Which ones built them up? Which do you want to choose?

Prayer: Lord Jesus, the Truth, the Way, and the Life, this Lent may we grow in speaking your truth, following your truth, and living your truth in love.

Rewriting the Story

Readings: Gen 2:7-9; 3:1-7; Rom 5:12-19 or 5:12, 17-19; Matt 4:1-11

Scripture:
Jesus was led by the Spirit into the desert
  to be tempted by the devil. (Matt 4:1)

Reflection: The story of Lent begins here, not with ashes but with the reason for them. It is a story of forgetting, remembering, and rewriting.

Genesis 3 recounts the primal tragedy of human forgetfulness. The Tempter offers Eve, with Adam standing by, a portrait of God skewed by a clever addition. The addition replaces the loving artisan of the opening chapters of Genesis with a lying God who forbids them access to the fruit of the tree not to prevent their death but to keep them from becoming like gods, that is, competitors. They accept the falsified portrait. Already they have forgotten the God whose fingerprints mark their clay and whose breath is their life. And they have forgotten who they were first made to be: not God's competitors but God's image (Gen 1:27-28).

The gospel tells the story of Jesus' remembering. Emerging from the Jordan as the beginning of God's new creation, he is driven into the desert. There he confronts the same Tempter. This trickster offers Jesus a skewed script of how he would behave if he really were the son of God. He would take quick, painless, and selfish shortcuts to reach his goal: feeding his own hunger, forcing God to prove love for him, and worshiping the tempter as a God-substitute who will make him instant ruler of the world with no exhausting ministry and no crucifixion. By implication, the true God is presented as an obstacle to Jesus' easy success. But Jesus is not heir to the original forgetfulness. He remembers clearly who God is and consequently who he is. And he recognizes the falsified picture for what it is and refuses it.

Jesus is rewriting our story. We have all had some experience of the Tempter offering us fool's gold in place of the real thing. We have all been presented with a subtly falsified portrait of God and thus of ourselves. But Jesus offers us a new script for the confrontation: fidelity to God's word. Jesus' script invites us during Lent to collaborate in rewriting our own story, replacing the false with the true.

Meditation: What do your temptations tell you about yourself and about God? Where do they falsify God's identity and yours?

Prayer: O God of truth, grant us the grace this Lent to recognize temptations to forgetfulness and to rewrite our stories by the light of God's word.

The Holiness Program

Readings: Lev 19:1-2, 11-18; Matt 25:31-46

Scripture:
"Be holy, for I, the LORD, your God, am holy." (Lev 19:2)

Reflection: What could it possibly mean for God to say in the same breath, "Be holy" and "I am holy"? We sometimes hear God's holiness defined as otherness. No wonder we then enthrone holy people on pillars, eyes cast heavenward, hands joined in prayer, untroubled by the world around them—and a safe distance from us. Mother Cabrini up to her elbows in troubled immigrants, or Mother Teresa collecting the dying from the streets, or Maximilian Kolbe taking a family man's place in a starvation bunker would certainly laugh at that picture!

Yet holiness is dangerous. God, the Holy One of Israel, ordered Moses to keep his distance and take off his shoes on the holy ground before the burning bush. Only the high priest was admitted into God's presence in the holy of holies in the Jerusalem temple. God claimed divine otherness and distance through Isaiah: "For as the heavens are higher than the earth, / so are my ways higher than your ways, / my thoughts higher than your thoughts" (Isa 55:9).

What, then, could we have in common with the all-holy God? Vatican II spelled out the link in the Dogmatic Constitution on the Church (*Lumen Gentium*): All are called to holiness in "the perfection of charity," that is, love undistorted by self-seeking. And "God is love" (1 John 4:8).

Keeping this notion of holiness vague is a great way to escape its demands. God won't let us get away with it. The first reading from a section of the book of Leviticus titled "the Holiness Code" (Lev 17–26) spells out concretely some of what holiness looks like: Don't steal, cheat, oppress, or harm anyone. Give up hatred, revenge, and grudges. The picture is summed up in a commandment we know well: "You shall love your neighbor as yourself" (Mark 12:31). That's an effective twist: Would you do any of these things to yourself?

Jesus adds yet another twist: whatever you do, or don't do, to those in need, you do, or don't do, to him.

We could close the Lenten Lectionary right here. This is program enough to occupy us for many Lents, for a lifetime in fact. And so it must.

Meditation: Read the list of holiness requirements prayerfully. Do any of them speak to you?

Prayer: All Holy God, make us holy in loving you and our neighbor.

No Empty Words

Readings: Isa 55:10-11; Matt 6:7-15

Scripture:
[My word] shall not return to me void,
   but shall do my will,
   achieving the end for which I sent it. (Isa 55:11)

Reflection: Prayer is a central Lenten work. Today, Jesus teaches his disciples—us—the most beloved of all prayer: "Our Father, who art in heaven . . ." Do you remember when you learned it? I was four or five when my grandmother taught it to me as I knelt beside my bed. But, being Presbyterian, she taught me to ask forgiveness for debts as I forgave my debtors, whoever they were. Later, in Catholic school, I learned that the debts were really trespasses, which weren't a whole lot clearer. Sister Stanislaus tried to simplify it: "That means 'sins,' children. You know what sins are." Presbyterian-raised and Catholic-educated, I certainly did.

But the point of this ancient prayer is not the exact words, treasured though they are in Christian experience. Otherwise, why would God have given us two differing versions, one in Matthew and one in Luke? The point of any version is connection and transformation.

This often-prayed text seeps into our bones with use. When we are tired, lost, or simply numb with routine, we murmur "Our Father," and the rest of the words tumble out around us and shelter us, like the stone walls of a sheepfold. God is there. We are connected. A chaplain told of praying with a patient deep in dementia. At the Our Father, the patient, who hadn't been speaking, joined in. The phrases were familiar. They were home. They were ties to the God who never forgets even when we do.

But the words we make so much our own are not ours to start with. They are God's. Over time, we invest them with bits of ourselves—anxiety over a loved one's surgery, tears prompted by a child at prayer, sudden recognition when our refusal to forgive is blocking God's desire to forgive us. As we murmur them, these words of God return to the sender, bearing our lives with them. God accepts them and transforms us to fit the prayer.

So, in darkness and light, danger and safe harbor, fervor and boredom, let us carry these words back to God laden with our lives as they are, knowing the gift is always welcomed and made new.

Meditation: Pray the Lord's Prayer very slowly and reflectively, linking it to your own life.

Prayer: Christ, teach us always to pray!

Signs of Mercy

Readings: John 3:1-10; Luke 11:29-32

Scripture:
  "This generation is an evil generation;
  it seeks a sign, but no sign will be given it,
  except the sign of Jonah." (Luke 11:29)

Reflection: Everyone knew the Ninevites weren't worth preaching to. Jonah, the prophet sent to convert them, knew it. Jesus' hearers knew it. They were *pagans*, for heaven's sake! Worse, Nineveh, capital of ancient Assyria, was The Enemy, or had been in its heyday when its armies invaded the northern kingdom of Israel and carried off most of the inhabitants. Admittedly, that was centuries before Jesus, but his contemporaries still lived unhappily cheek by jowl with the Samaritans, descendants of the mixed population of native Israelite and alien imports the Assyrians created at the time. Everybody knew there was no converting a Samaritan, never mind an Assyrian!

Jesus pointed out the awkward fact that Jonah's call to repent and be saved did just that. Everyone from the Assyrian king on down to the littlest kitchen slave put on sackcloth and ashes. Everyone down to the cook's cat fasted. They gave up their wickedness, ceased smiting their enemies, and prayed God would forgive them. And God did.

The book of Jonah is generally considered fiction, but a good story is a good story. This one makes us wonder. What about those terrorists, those racial supremacists, those people next door we've always thought irredeemable? Unlike ourselves, of course. We're good Christians, after all. Aren't we?

We'd appreciate some sign that Jesus agrees, but he promises his hearers, and us, one sign only: the sign of Jonah. In Luke's account, that sign is Jonah's successful mission to those undeserving Ninevites. Perhaps we'd best turn to the responsorial psalm refrain: "A heart contrite and humbled, O God, you will not spurn." That, Jesus seems to say, is what counts.

Better line up with the Ninevites, then, and take the Lenten call to repentance and conversion to heart. Literally.

Meditation: Lent is the season of mercy, the season when we can look in the biblical mirror and see ourselves as we are. Do you see anything in the mirror that calls for any change on your part?

Prayer: God of mercy and compassion, heal us of our hidden pride and grant us the humility to accept your gift of conversion in this season.

March 9: Thursday of the First Week of Lent

Ask, Seek, Knock

Readings: Esth C:12, 14-16, 23-25; Matt 7:7-12

Scripture:
"Ask and it will be given to you;
seek and you will find;
knock and the door will be opened to you." (Matt 7:7)

Reflection: There is nothing more disappointing than asking someone you love for something that never comes, seeking those you care for only to see them turn away, knocking at their door only to be left standing outside. As we take to heart the Lenten encouragement to pray, we can find comfort in today's assurance that when we ask, God will give, when we seek, God will let us find, when we knock, God will open the door.

But this passage always seems to me to hold a hidden poignancy. It is God's unspoken questions: When I ask, will you give *me* a stone or a loaf of bread? When I seek, will you come running, or will you hide? When I knock on your door, will you answer?

We might defend ourselves with counter questions: Lord, when did you ask? When did you seek? When did you knock? The simple answer is: always. The deeper answer is: listen to your heart. What does it tell you?

Lent offers a good opportunity to grow in discernment, the art of paying attention to all those inner voices that clamor for our attention and learning to catch God's voice among them. A brief inspiration, an unexpected thought, a tug on the sleeve of the spirit that says, "Come to me!" or "How about taking a prayer break?" or "Did you ever think about this?" Lent encourages us to pay closer attention to the needs and desires of others around us, but do we ever take time to reflect on God's desires?

We want *God* to listen, to give what we ask for, to provide what we seek, to answer at our knock. But reread the last line of today's gospel in this light: "Do to *others* whatever you would have *them* do to *you*." And God is one of the others. Love's door opens both ways.

Meditation: How does God catch your attention? Consider making it a practice to look back over the day or week and take note of what God has asked of you, how God has sought to be found, when God has knocked at your door.

Prayer: Giver of all good gifts, grant us hearts grateful for all your goodness to us and attentive to all that you ask of us, so that we may grow in love of you.

Farther Steps

Readings: Ezek 18:21-28; Matt 5:20-26

Scripture:
"[U]nless your righteousness surpasses that
of the scribes and Pharisees,
you will not enter into the Kingdom of heaven."
(Matt 5:20)

Reflection: Scribes and Pharisees often appear in the gospels as Jesus' adversaries. In today's gospel, he does not contradict their traditional teaching, based on the commandment forbidding killing: "You shall not kill; and whoever kills will be liable to judgment" (cf. Exod 20:13; Deut 5:17). But he urges his hearers to take it two steps farther: give up angry insults and verbal assaults, whether or not they lead to physical violence; and make it up with the one who has angered you—or whom you have hurt. So important does Jesus consider this reconciliation that he gives it priority over worship.

This gospel passage follows rather curiously on the heels of God's insistence, through Ezekiel, that the wicked who change their ways will be saved, but the good who turn to sin will perish. Jesus argues with the scribes and Pharisees, gets frustrated with them, and accuses them of hypocrisy. He warns that their righteous observance of the law is not enough to gain them entry into the kingdom of heaven. At the same time, in this verse he sets the standard for his own treatment of these obstreperous opponents. Behind his anger with them lies grief at their hardness of heart (Mark 3:5). Where we might be tempted to harm those who stand against us, Jesus seems to want above all what God desires for the sinners in Ezekiel 18: that they open their hearts, recognize their wrongheadedness, and change their ways. In other words, through all his contention with them he seems to passionately seek their conversion and reconciliation with God. To them, he is the dangerous blasphemer who must be stopped. To him, they are his brothers.

Meditation: Think of three people you disapprove of and often disagree with—or who disapprove of you and disagree with you, perhaps heatedly. What do you desire for them?

Prayer: Jesus, you are the human face of God's mercy. Teach us to become the same.

March 11: Saturday of the First Week of Lent

Image and Likeness

Readings: Deut 26:16-19; Matt 5:43-48

Scripture:
"So be perfect, just as your heavenly Father is perfect."
  (Matt 5:48)

Reflection: There it is again: be like God! We met this command last Monday.

The word "perfect" usually stops us in our tracks. "Perfect? Me? No way!" Or the perfectionists among us might grumble that every effort to get over trying to be perfect was just thrown out the window. And by no less an authority than Jesus!

We could detour through the thicket of interpretations of "perfect," but for now let's just admit that Jesus has outdone himself in commanding the impossible.

Or has he? Perhaps Jesus is looking at a bigger picture than we are. He is remembering what we so often forget: we are in fact created in the image and likeness of God. He is asking us to become again what we were made to be: just like God. But the Genesis author knew God primarily as creator. Jesus tells us to concentrate now on the fact that God is, above all else, love (1 John 4:8). Then he says that our old pictures of love are sadly out of focus, so we are too. We may pat ourselves on the back for the way we love our parents, spouse, children, and friends in a world where so many can't even manage that. Not enough, says Jesus. Loving the lovable is certainly a good thing, but God does not stop there. God loves all human beings without exception, even those who return the divine love with indifference, hatred, or ridicule. And therefore so must we. Jesus, the true image of God, will give us the supreme example from the cross, when he asks the Father to forgive "them"—his tormentors, his mockers, but also all sinful humanity (Luke 23:34).

Before we back off, shaking our heads at the mere thought that we could be that kind of perfect, let us remember that we are bonded with Christ at our deepest core through baptism, so we never love by our own effort only but always in, with, and through him. We can become perfect by living our baptismal identity fully—and that is our Lenten hope and aim, year by year.

Meditation: Who would you rather not try to love? Who might rather not try to love you? Can you imagine how God loves both them and you?

Prayer: God of love, break down in us all the boundaries we have set to our love so that in Christ, we may love as you love.

Mountain Climbing

Readings: Gen 12:1-4a; 2 Tim 1:8b-10; Matt 17:1-9

Scripture:
Jesus took Peter, James, and John his brother,
    and led them up a high mountain by themselves.
And he was transfigured before them;
    his face shone like the sun
    and his clothes became white as light. (Matt 17:1-2)

Reflection: Have you ever noticed how often Jesus goes up the mountain to pray? No wonder. In Scripture, the mountain is God's reserved place, so through the prophets God railed at faithless Israel for worshiping false gods in the high places (e.g., Jer 32:35). The most important high places for the worship of the true God became Mount Sinai, where God appeared to Moses and later to Elijah, and Mount Zion, site of Jerusalem and its great temple (1 Kgs 8:1-2; 2 Chr 5:2; Ps 24). Those high places became the prime sites for Israel's encounters with God.

People still choose mountain retreats as places of prayer. Mountains offer silent refuge from the deafening clamor of the marketplace to allow the heart to hear God's voice. Clear mountain air and far horizons allow one to see God and God's work in perspective.

But the high places endanger complacency. Jesus takes his three closest followers to the mountaintop and there reveals to them more truth than they can bear. On Tabor, he speaks with Moses, voice of the law, and Elijah, voice of the prophets, almost as God once did on Sinai. Jesus has the appearance of one bathed in blinding light—and to the biblical mind, fire, the only source of light then known, is God's robe, concealing and revealing the divine holiness. God's voice confirms that Jesus is God's son, though believers would spend ages unraveling what that meant. The disciples are overwhelmed.

Jesus warns them, though, to say nothing. The picture is not yet complete. Between the transfiguration on one mountain and the ascension from another lie the Mount of Olives, site of Jesus' agony, and Mount Calvary, site of Jesus' death. Only the resurrection will reconcile all the mountain revelations into the one reality of Jesus Christ dead, risen, and forever robed in unimaginable glory at God's right hand.

Lent invites us to follow Christ by climbing each of these mountains—Tabor, Olivet, and Calvary—and on each to discover more fully who Christ is and who we are to become in him.

Meditation: Reflect on the transfiguration (Mount Tabor), the agony in the garden (Mount Olivet), and the crucifixion (Mount Calvary). What does each one teach you about Jesus? How does each one invite you to enter into a deeper relationship with him in your own experiences of self-revelation, hesitation, and self-giving in suffering?

Prayer: Lord Jesus, take us with you up the mountains of your suffering and glory to pray and to know you more truly.

March 13: Monday of the Second Week of Lent

Empty Space

Readings: Dan 9:4b-10; Luke 6:36-38

Scripture:
"For the measure with which you measure
   will in turn be measured out to you." (Luke 6:38)

Reflection: The word "Lent" comes from a Middle English root meaning "springtime." Lenten asceticism looks like spring cleaning. We clean out our cupboards and give our surplus food to the local food pantry or soup kitchen. We clean out our closets and drawers and give clothes we no longer wear to Goodwill or the Salvation Army. Look at all that empty space! Now, turn off one TV program a day, or one video game, or one hour of social media time. There! Empty time to match that empty space!

But emptiness seems to frighten a consumer culture and perhaps us, its creators and denizens. An image from a British mystery novel comes to my mind. In a moment of enlightenment, the protagonist says of a demanding houseguest, "Beatrice's pleasures, I saw, were a way of passing time that had no other purpose: a vista of smothering pointlessness . . . No wonder, I thought, that she complained, with all that void pursuing her."

Jesus seems to insist that we not stop with emptying pantries or clothes closets or even hours in the day but that we empty our hearts. He tells us, "Throw out all those judgments you keep making of other peoples' words and actions, appearance and motives. Take your burden of condemnations to the rubbish heap. (And don't look for others to whom to pass them on!) Pack up that accumulation of grievances, resentments, grudges, and put them on the curb with the trash. Now, look at all that inner space you have!"

Don't let that void pursue you into gathering up new materials for judgment, condemnation, and unforgivingness. Instead, just let it be. Our merciful God will fill the space you've emptied with understanding, compassion, and love. In other words, Easter life!

Meditation: Consider making this Lent a progressive spring cleaning, outwardly and inwardly. Start with the material goods you could give away and move on to the internal "junk" that clutters your spirit with negativities.

Prayer: God, giver of all good gifts, free us from the burden of too many and too much; free us of the inner burden of judgments and unforgiven hurts; free us to rejoice in gratitude for renewed hearts at Easter.

Live It as It Is!

Readings: Isa 1:10, 16-20; Matt 23:1-12

Scripture:
"All their works are performed to be seen." (Matt 23:5)

Reflection: Jesus challenges us to take a new look at "scribes and Pharisees," religious spin artists then and now. "All their works are performed to be seen." The works Jesus names—widening phylacteries and lengthening tassels, for instance—mean nothing to most of us, but we might recognize them in modern Christian dress as wearing ostentatious crosses and holding Bibles or rosaries clearly in hand for others to notice. Jesus has no objection to genuine tools of piety. His concern is with religious practices ruled by that ruinous principle old and new: image is everything.

And when he speaks about the scribes and Pharisees, he's looking at his own followers, including us. Mind you, he always looks with understanding, reading the hearts behind the religious posturing. He recognizes when the posturing is the pride of the Pharisee who thanked God in the temple for his superior holiness over unacceptable sinners (Luke 18:11). But he also knows when posturing is armor assumed to mask the fear that we might actually be one of those sinners God could never find acceptable. One hears it said that the hardest thing for most Christians to believe is that God really loves each and every one of us. In that case, the phylacteries and tassels, the large crosses and visible Bibles and rosaries are much more to convince ourselves (and maybe even God!) than to persuade others that we are worth something in God's eyes.

Don't do it, Jesus says. Drop all the pretenses and disguises, put away the jewelry. "Whoever exalts himself will be humbled; / but whoever humbles himself will be exalted" (Matt 23:12). But, as we've heard, humility is truth. So own your own truth, Jesus seems to say. Own it with all its glories and warts intact. Stand before yourself and before God without pretense. The results might surprise you, because when God stands as God is before us as we are, it becomes clearer than ever that God is, in fact, love.

Meditation: Do you really believe deep down that God loves you? If yes, give thanks. If not, ask yourself what you see as insurmountable obstacles to God's love and ask God if that's true.

Prayer: God of truth, grant us the grace to know and to believe in your love for us as we are and to allow that love to transform us into the people you have made us to become.

True Service

Readings: Jer 18:18-20; Matt 20:17-28

Scripture:
"[T]he Son of Man did not come to be served but to serve and to give his life as a ransom for many." (Matt 20:28)

Reflection: Up till now, the Lectionary has been a textbook for our Lenten study of the baptismal commitment we will accept or renew at Easter. We've reviewed some of the tools for our transformation into a more vivid image of God in Christ. We've heard what that could look like. But today's readings provide a sobering preview of what is required beyond praying, fasting, giving alms, and trying to live holy lives. The readings offer one picture only: Jesus Christ walking willingly into enemy fire to pick up and redeem all those who have been and will be felled by it. This Jesus is not a pretty picture: he is judged, condemned, mocked, scourged, and crucified before he is raised on the third day.

In the gospel, Jesus quickly draws back and lets the curtain fall again over that horrifying vision of the book's penultimate chapter. Instead, confronted by the ambitions of the Zebedee family, mother and sons, he uses the gentler imagery of a chalice to be drunk. We know what it is: we will come again soon to the story of the chalice Jesus will find too much but will accept anyway and drink down on our behalf (Mark 14:35-36). But for now we are spared the details as Jesus recasts the story of suffering and death into the story of service. Ah, now that's a comfortable theme for Lenten Christians, isn't it? Until, of course, Jesus adds the zinger at the end: ultimately the service we're called to is the same as his—to give up our lives for others, though that will more likely be by self-sacrificing service than by death.

Lent is living toward the cross in such a way that, when it opens like a door before us as it did for Jesus, though in different ways, we will walk through willingly, not for our sakes but for the sake of all those he gave his life to save.

Meditation: Think about the hard moments you've already known in your efforts to be of real service to others. What made them hard? When did they deter you from your desire to serve and when did they not?

Prayer: Crucified and risen Lord, so shape us through this Lent that whenever the cross invites us in, we will embrace it gladly for love of those you love.

Later

Readings: Jer 17:5-10; Luke 16:19-31

Scripture:
"The rich man also died and was buried . . ."
   (Luke 16:22)

Reflection: Lent warns us again and again that "later" may be too late. The story of the rich man and the poor beggar Lazarus repeats the warning.

The rich man was not a bad person, just a wealthy one inattentive to a neighbor's need. Given time, he might eventually have noticed the daily suppliant at his door. Maybe one of the dogs would have snarled at him and caught his attention. He was given time, a lifetime, but it wasn't enough. And suddenly, it was too late. After death, he realizes the opportunity he has lost, or rather thrown away on his own daily feasts, so he begs Abraham to send Lazarus back from the dead to warn his brothers. Too late, too late, says Abraham, too many warnings already unheeded, even when given by Moses and the prophets. The rich man apparently does love his brothers and pleads that Lazarus, raised from the dead, should startle them enough to get their minds onto essentials. But no, it is already too late. The habit of the deaf ear has grown too strong to break. We can hardly miss the irony of that ending told by Jesus, who will in fact return from the dead and, all too often, still go unheard by those busy about more pressing (i.e., selfish) business.

This story bothers me. I do "later" very well. Every year, I have heard St. Paul's urgent Ash Wednesday warning: "behold, now is the day of salvation" (2 Cor 6:2). And every year, I do diligently make serious Lenten efforts, but every year, come Easter, I let go of the season's unfinished business, the places in the heart as yet unconvinced and unconverted, sing my alleluias, and go on about life as usual—a bit reformed, I hope, but still too often ignoring the beggars on my doorstep, whatever form they take, because I'm busy meeting some other deadline than the Lord's, until next Lent. The rich man always stops me in my tracks for a moment, though. What if there is no "next Lent"? Or what if I have grown too deaf to hear its warning when it comes?

Meditation: List three good works you have been putting off, three "beggars at your door." What stops you from attending to them now?

Prayer: God of time and timelessness, awaken us from the sloth of "later" to the urgency of today crying out for our attention and care.

Really?

Readings: Gen 37:3-4, 12-13a, 17b-28a; Matt 21:33-43, 45-46

Scripture:
"This is the heir.
Come, let us kill him and acquire his inheritance."
(Matt 21:38)

Reflection: The first reading tells of Joseph of the many-colored coat and jealous brothers. The gospel tells of a land-owner and avaricious tenants. It's the same story of tunnel vision told twice, with only the names changed to identify the guilty. In both cases, the guilty parties become fixated on themselves to the exclusion of all else, even common sense, and determine to get rid of the competition. Not an unfamiliar agenda in our own day!

In the first story, the brothers, aware of their father's preference for Joseph, brood and mutter among themselves about how to solve the problem. Finally, they decide to kill Joseph. Why? What do they expect? That Jacob will forget about Joseph and divide his love among all of them equally? Really? In the second story, the landowner works to create a vineyard, and then leases it to tenants while he travels. When the tenants beat or kill the servants sent to collect the rent, the exasperated owner finally sends his own son. And they decide to kill him too so they can keep the vineyard for themselves. Again, really? The bereaved owner will just give it to them? And they won't turn on one another to get rid of the competition?

Let's take a look at those brothers and tenants because they have something to teach us about how not to live Lent. Lenten asceticism is easily confused with self-improvement, especially religious self-improvement. Our goal can become the good not of God and neighbor but of ourselves. We can even be tempted to eliminate the competition for God's approval by making the competitors look small—criticizing the daily Mass-goer for being hard on employees afterward, or sneering at someone at the daily rosary for scolding the kids in the parking lot, or magnifying flaws in parish clergy or pastoral ministers lest they look holier than we do. Really? God's approval is in limited supply? And we'll get more of it if others get less?

Let's not be so foolish. Let's be glad for Joseph, work hard in the vineyard for the owner's profit, and live our Lenten resolutions for God's glory, not ours.

Meditation: Whom do you often criticize? Why? How do you imagine your criticism rings in God's ear?

Prayer: God, giver of all gifts, free us from our petty jealousies before they can consume us. Let us work faithfully to achieve your goals rather than our own.

March 18: Saturday of the Second Week of Lent

Prodigal Mercy

Readings: Mic 7:14-15, 18-20; Luke 15:1-3, 11-32

Scripture:
Who is there like you, the God who removes guilt
and pardons sin for the remnant of his inheritance;
Who does not persist in anger forever,
but delights rather in clemency,
And will again have compassion on us,
treading underfoot our guilt? (Mic 7:18-19)

Reflection: Let's face it. That younger son is a selfish, manipulative little twit. With visions of wine, women, and song dancing in his hand, he demands his inheritance. No thought of what this will do to the family finances, what land his father will have to sell off to realize that much cash, how anyone will feel about his decision to take off. And off he does go, into a life of careless debauchery with no thought for tomorrow. When tomorrow comes, he finds himself alone, sober by necessity, and broke. Now the spoiled heir has to go to work feeding pigs, not a desirable entry-level job for the child of a people who consider pork unclean food. Unhappy and hungry, he sits down to calculate his options. OK, he says to himself, I'd better go home to Dad. But what is he really looking for? It sounds like what he wants is really a good meal, and more good meals to come. The only lesson he has learned, it seems, is that hunger hurts.

It doesn't matter to the father. All he wants is to have his boy home safe. He will have time then to do a better job of teaching him to be a real family member with his eyes on a greater good than himself.

And it doesn't matter to God. Any motive will do as a starting place. Jesus often appeals to our self-interest as a beginning motive to live the gospel (e.g., Luke 14:7-10, 25-33). What matters is that our Lenten practices bring us home from the places where all of us stray in our selfishness, albeit not necessarily as dramatically as the kid in the parable, so that, close to God again, we can still learn to give and share rather than take.

Meditation: What draws you "home" to Christ? Some of your motives may be self-focused, but the deeper ones will look beyond yourself. Try to identify some of both.

Prayer: God of mercy, free us from all that keeps us in places far from you and draw us to yourself.

Water Bearer

Readings: Exod 17:3-7; Rom 5:1-2, 5-8; John 4:5-42 or John 4:5-15, 19b-26, 39a, 40-42

Scripture:
"[T]he water I shall give will become . . .
a spring of water welling up to eternal life." (John 4:14)

Reflection: In the context of Lent, Exodus offers a preview of Jesus' crucifixion. God tells Moses that the Divine Presence will stand before him on the rock in the desert and that Moses must strike the rock with his rod to release water that will save the thirsting people's lives.

St. Paul will later say that this rock is Christ (1 Cor 10:3). Jesus, seated by the Samaritan well, promises the woman he meets there that "the water I shall give will become [in whoever drinks it] / a spring of water welling up to eternal life." What he gives to her is not a drink of water but only his word. The biblical imagination often pictures God's word as living water (cf. Ps 1:2-3). Commentators hear in Jesus' words an echo of God's promise in Isaiah 12:3, "With joy you will draw water / from the fountains of salvation."

But to drink his word, one must be prepared for a strong dose. It is a word of truth. Jesus tells the woman exactly what she has been up to—marriage after marriage, and then life with a man to whom she is not married. Notice that the woman does not flinch. She hides behind no denials or excuses. On the contrary, she embraces everything Jesus has to say about her and then about himself with joyful excitement.

But we will have to wait for John's account of the crucifixion to discover the real source of the life-giving water Jesus offers. On Good Friday we will hear that when a soldier strikes the dead Jesus with a spear, "blood and water flowed out" (John 19:34). In the 1959 movie *Ben-Hur*, it is raining at the time. In a powerful image, the blood flows down the wood and mingles with pools of rainwater in the stony ground and flows out everywhere. The word of life is released into the world.

Meditation: Today we remember that the great baptismal feast of Easter lies only weeks ahead. The waters of baptism flow from the cross. What does that word of truth about God and about ourselves require of us?

Prayer: Jesus, source and bearer of the word of life, teach us to recognize our thirst and to welcome your word of truth with the honesty of the Samaritan woman.

Between One Day and the Next

Readings: 2 Sam 7:4-5a, 12-14a, 16; Rom 4:13, 16-18, 22; Matt 1:16, 18-21, 24a or Luke 2:41-51a

Scripture:
[Joseph] did as the angel of the Lord had commanded him . . . (Matt 1:24)

Reflection: Between one day and the next, Joseph's world turns upside down. One day he is betrothed to a virgin in the town of Nazareth. The next, he is betrothed to a woman found to be pregnant with a child not his. The only explanation is infidelity. The news leaves a righteous man's clearly regulated world standing on its head, and he with it. All he can do is choose between disgracing Mary in public, possibly at the price of her death, and divorcing her privately, perhaps for exile with relatives far away. Neither choice offers anything but misery for Joseph, but he chooses the private divorce to protect her.

Then, between one day and the next, Joseph's world turns upside down again. One day, he is betrothed to a woman pregnant but with a child not his, faced with two painful ways to end their relationship. The next, he is betrothed to a woman pregnant with a child conceived in her by the Holy Spirit. The angel's news leaves a righteous but compassionate man's clearly regulated world standing on its head, and he with it. Once again he has to choose: take Mary into his home as his fully accepted wife, as the angel commanded? Or dismiss the dream as wishful hallucination and divorce her anyway? Neither choice offers him much comfort. He chooses the first because he believes God has asked it, although no one has explained it, or could.

Between one day and the next, Joseph has no time for prolonged reflection and no clear guidelines to aid discernment. It doesn't matter. For Joseph there has always been one choice only. In this, he and Mary are of one mind and heart: "May it be done to me according to your word" (Luke 1:38). Here is the very essence of Lent in a single sentence.

Meditation: When presented with a choice for which God provides no reasonable explanations, what have you done in the past? What was the outcome? What will you do next time?

Prayer: St. Joseph, man of few words but God's, teach us to listen deeply for God's will and obey.

The Arithmetic of Mercy

Readings: Dan 3:25, 34-43; Matt 18:21-35

Scripture:
Peter approached Jesus and asked him,
  "Lord, . . . how often must I forgive him?
As many as seven times?"
Jesus answered, "I say to you, not seven times but seventy-
  seven times." (Matt 18:22)

Reflection: Peter learned his arithmetic from an outdated textbook. Having heard "an eye for an eye," he probably thought his proposal to forgive an offending brother seven times would earn him a gold star. But Jesus was writing a new textbook where the correct answer was "not seven times but seventy-seven times," meaning "Don't even count."

Peter's jaw must have dropped, so Jesus told a story about a king and a servant with a debt so huge no servant could pay it. The king's solution: recoup some of the loss by selling the servant, his family, and his property. The servant pleads: given time, he will pay the whole debt. His is the wild arithmetic of desperation we still hear from modern debtors pleading for extensions on a loan, a mortgage, a car payment. Of course their creditors know nothing of the arithmetic of mercy. The king in the story, "moved with compassion," does: he remits the debt entirely.

Who is this king? Does Jesus really mean to paint a picture of God the Great Pushover, doling out forgiveness to anyone who begs hard enough, no matter what the sin? And forgiveness with no strings attached at that: the slave goes away with his slate wiped clean. That sounds like an invitation to happy profligacy: you can do whatever you want, as long as you go to confession and ask nicely for absolution. Oh yeah, you do have to say you're sorry, but that's easy enough.

Jesus pours cold water on equating mercy with blind folly. No, he says, there is a limit to God's mercy, but only one. The forgiven servant goes out and beats the stuffing out of a fellow servant who owes him a far tinier sum, even though he no longer needs the repayment to cover his own debt to the king. The king sends the unforgiving servant to debtors' prison. Mercy received must equal mercy given, says Jesus. When you experience the stupendous mercy of God, there is only one arithmetically correct answer: go and do likewise!

Meditation: The first reading is a plea for God's forgiveness but it comes at the price of forgiving others. What do you want forgiven? What are you called to forgive?

Prayer: O God of mercy, grant us the humility and love to forgive those who wrong us and to forgive ourselves when we wrong our own ideals and hopes.

More than Rules

Readings: Deut 4:1, 5-9; Matt 5:17-19

Scripture:
"I have come not to abolish but to fulfill [the law]."
   (Matt 5:17)

Reflection: Rules can either chafe or reassure. They chafe when we hanker after unrestricted freedom. They reassure when we want security in a world of growing chaos. In either case, they are boxes. God's commandments, on the other hand, are means.

God has never much liked being boxed. We sometimes picture the God of the Israelites' desert housed in the special box we call "the ark of the covenant," but it was the tablets of the law and other holy relics that rode in the box. The Divine Presence hovered above it or moved on ahead. Even today, while we reverence the Real Presence of Christ in the eucharistic species housed in the tabernacle, we know perfectly well that Christ is not confined there. He is everywhere and always with us, though very differently in the crowded subway, on the beach, or in the quiet of our prayer corner than in the Blessed Sacrament.

Why, then, would this unboxed God impose commandments on us to box us in? God didn't, and they don't. Jesus can say he came to fulfill the law for very good reason. God's law is an instruction book on how to become fully human, undistorted by sin. The book acquired several chapters over time: the Ten Commandments given on Sinai, the supplementary law expanded in the books of Exodus and Leviticus, and rabbinic glosses added to connect ancient law with contemporary experience in the time of Jesus and later. Jesus denied none of the biblical law, but he boiled it down to the two essentials: "You shall love the Lord, your God, with all your heart, with all your soul, and with all your mind. . . . You shall love your neighbor as yourself" (Matt 22:37-39). Then you will be the images of the God of love you were meant to be.

And he lived what he taught. He is the law of God embodied in human flesh (cf. John 1:14) and untainted by any self-interest, so he is the true image of God (cf. Col 1:15; Heb 1:3) and our teacher.

The laws of God are no box, then. They cramp and chafe our selfishness, but not our true humanity. Rather they protect and guide us till we get there.

Meditation: What do God's commandments teach you about true human beings and communities? How do they describe you?

Prayer: Lord Jesus, fulfillment of God's law, make us the new humanity you model and achieve for us through your death and resurrection.

March 23: Thursday of the Third Week of Lent

Confusing the Source

Readings: Jer 7:23-28; Luke 11:14-23

Scripture:
This is the nation that does not listen
to the voice of the LORD, its God,
or take correction. (Jer 7:28)

Reflection: God's judgment sounds harsh on Jeremiah's tongue, but Jesus' opponents in the gospel bear witness to its truth. They don't listen to Jesus' voice for very good reason: they have mistaken its source. If you identify a speaker as evil's representative, then you have excellent grounds for not listening to him. Instead, you can stand up to him and dismiss him courageously and imagine yourself a very good, religious person indeed.

By this time, Jesus has amassed an impressive track record of wresting people from suffering sickness and handicap, misunderstanding God's law, doing harm to their neighbors, and otherwise living under the reign not of God but of evil. Yet his opponents dismiss it entirely by claiming that he gets all his power from a frightening taskmaster: Beelzebul, prince of demons. Jesus points out the fallacy in their logic, but he knows very well it will do no good. Determined deafness does not respond to logical argument.

The scene makes me wonder, not about Jesus but about myself as a listener. An honest listener is open to correction and change, but am I? When I was the impassioned teenage advocate of all sorts of causes not well thought out, my father would counter with calm logic based on fact until I had no place to go except out of the room, usually in a cloud of righteous temper. I have learned since that defensiveness is rarely the posture of a genuine listener, but I still sometimes summon up bad logic to defend poorly chosen ideas and actions. I wonder whose voice I am shutting out then, and to whose voice I am listening. I would be afraid to ask the prophet Jeremiah, if he dropped by, because I'm afraid I know what his answer would be.

Meditation: When have you found yourself most likely to shut out the voice of God with irrational—but loud—arguments? What has provoked your defensiveness?

Prayer: O God of mercy, heal us of the deafness we choose as the armor of wrongheaded self-defense and grant us the grace of hearts willing to hear the voice of your truth seeking to guide us to life.

Words

Readings: Hos 14:2-10; Mark 12:28-34

Scripture:
Take with you words,
    and return to the LORD . . . (Hos 14:2)

Reflection: Words aren't usually enough. Jesus is hard on people who substitute cries of "Lord, Lord" for action (Matt 7:21). Ah, but the *right* words: that's different.

The prophet Hosea tells the faithless Israelites, "Take with you words, / and return to the LORD." What words? He makes a list: a plea for forgiveness, prayer offering sacrifice, renunciation of past words addressed to false gods—but the key item is the last one. It's a change of words signifying a change of heart. "We shall say no more, 'Our god,' / to the work of our hands." The surrounding pagan nations often honored as gods those handmade stone figures and bronze figurines that depicted power, ferocity, or fertility—none of which they possessed. But of the God of Israel alone it can be said, "in you the orphan finds compassion." The title "God" shifts from meaning powers who vanquish all opponents to One who offers deep concern for the smallest and least.

Jesus proposes a similar language shift. When asked to identify the first of all commandments, he says nothing about honoring God's almighty power as the one true ruler over all. Instead, he identifies as greatest the commandment to love God with all you've got in you and to love your neighbor as yourself (see Mark 12:29-31). The God of power invites only fear. The God of compassion invites love.

The scribe who asked about the greatest commandment understands. Love is the greatest worship there is, better even than burnt offerings. And Jesus compliments him: "You are not far from the Kingdom of God."

When you recognize that, like Israel of old, you have let a great gap open between yourself and God, don't widen it out of fear of God's power or God's holiness, though God is both powerful and holy. Instead, put words in the basket of offerings you carry in your arms and go right up to God. The words? Really, only a handful are necessary: "I'm sorry" and "I love you."

Meditation: When you think "God," what are the first three words that come to your mind? Is love one of them? Is it at the top of the list? If not, why not?

Prayer: Word of God made flesh, our Lord Jesus Christ, speak to us and in us and through us the words of your love.

A Meeting of Words

Readings: Isa 7:10-14; 8:10; Heb 10:4-10; Luke 1:26-38

Scripture:
"Behold, I am the handmaid of the Lord.
May it be done to me according to your word." (Luke 1:38)

Reflection: To this momentous meeting between the angel of God and the Virgin Mary, each comes bearing words. The angel brings God's life-changing words to Mary: "Behold, you will conceive in your womb and bear a son, / and you shall name him Jesus" (Luke 1:31). No extraneous explanations here, no softening of the blow to her own life plans, no excuses. Just the words. And, mysteriously, within them, behind them, through them, from them comes the Word to be spoken into flesh in her by the Spirit, the breath of God. All words are, after all, breath-borne.

Mary brings a lifetime—the years that have gone before, the years to come—wrapped up in a single phrase: "Behold, I am the handmaid of the Lord. / May it be done to me according to your word." She knows nothing less will do.

Reminding us of the prophet Hosea's message yesterday, the Letter to the Hebrews says, as if in her name and her Son's, "Sacrifices and offerings, / holocausts and sin offerings, / you neither desired nor delighted in. . . . Behold, I come to do your will."

It's a brief exchange, this conversation between Mary and the angel. The words are very few. But in that meeting of words the entire story of the world is rewritten. What was a chronicle of death has become a chronicle of life. And nothing has been the same since. Or will be.

Meditation: In the biblical world, words have power. What is said, by God or by human beings, happens, as in the encounter between the angel and the Virgin. In our world, words have been emptied of power, often meaning nothing and changing nothing. Think about words that have failed in your life: words of promise, words of commitment, words of conviction. Think about words that have succeeded in their purpose. What made the difference?

Prayer: Word of God made flesh in Mary, teach us to sift our words and grant us the fidelity to make them true.

Eyes of Wonder

Readings: 1 Sam 16:1b, 6-7, 10-13a; Eph 5:8-14; John 9:1-41 or John 9:1, 6-9, 13-17, 34-38

Scripture:
"He put clay on my eyes, and I washed, and now I can see." (John 9:15)

Reflection: In the deepest sense, we are all born blind. Within a few minutes of birth, our newly opened eyes see a kaleidoscope of surfaces, but we learn only slowly to see them as mother, lights, father, bed, kindly helper, doors, stranger. Full sight, grasping surfaces and relationships and meanings, takes time.

Today's gospel is a story of blindness before it is a story of sight. Jesus' ever-present antagonists are blind to all but surfaces: a Sabbath-breaker who makes outrageous claims, cleverly elusive parents, an argumentative man born blind. They don't like what they see. They will not see more because they refuse to open their eyes. Are they so afraid? Of what? Of a world beyond their understanding, a world that escapes their control, a new world that invites them to abandon fear and learn wonder? The man born without eyesight, on the other hand, sees beyond the surface. Anointed with clay and washed in water, he sees Jesus' face but at Jesus' instruction, he also sees the Son of Man, a messianic title. It must all overwhelm him but he plunges in because now he is unafraid of what he cannot understand or control. We don't know what happened to him after the story ends, but we can be sure he never closed the newly opened eyes of his heart to wonder unfolding around him. He would understand Rabbi Abraham Joshua Heschel: "Our goal should be to live life in radical amazement . . . get up in the morning and look at the world in a way that takes nothing for granted. . . . To be spiritual is to be amazed."

Baptism has been called "illumination" because it plunges us into Christ, the Light, through whom we see a world made new, and us with it. With the Light of the World to lead us, we are never confined to a world of surfaces too small and tight and well defined to allow us to be constantly amazed, taking nothing for granted, except the love God has for us.

Meditation: Ask Christ to open your eyes to see beyond the surface of the world around you. Look at someone you love. Look at someone you dislike. Look at someone you mistrust. Look slowly and prayerfully. What do you see that you have never seen before?

Prayer: Christ, Light of the World, open the eyes of our hearts to amazement, wonder, and faith-filled insight into the ordinary lit from within by your extraordinary light.

Words of Life

Readings: Isa 65:17-21; John 4:43-54

Scripture:
Jesus said to him, "You may go; your son will live."
(John 4:50)

Reflection: Last Friday's and Saturday's readings reminded us that we live immersed in words. The words that matter most are the words exchanged between God and human beings. God always speaks the word of power in truth. Today, then, we are invited to take seriously God's words reported by the prophet Isaiah: "Lo, I am about to create new heavens / and a new earth . . . No longer shall the sound of weeping be heard there, or the sound of crying." Yesterday's liturgy opened with the word "Rejoice." That joy has spilled over into Monday and all the days to follow.

On Saturday we celebrated the momentous exchange of words between the angel of God and the Virgin Mary, which began the story of the new heavens and the new earth. In today's readings, the story continues to unfold, centuries after the prophet's promise of joy, but only thirty odd years after the exchange in Nazareth. The bystander-reader looking from one to the other can see the joy rolling out from past to present. A royal official's son is on his deathbed. The grieving father begs Jesus urgently to come and cure him. Jesus doesn't have to. He says the words of promise —"your son will live"—and it happens. The father's weeping is stilled, his words of grief silenced, as the prophet had foretold.

We still live in the story's unfolding. The new heavens and the new earth, and the new humanity inhabiting them, are not yet completed. Chapters of death and grief remain to be written. But we will soon hear the story's climax, when death and life meet in mortal combat on the cross, and Life wins. All that comes after is merely the climax unfolding toward the last chapter of all, which we previewed in Isaiah and project into the book of Revelation. So, in the very teeth of death and loss and weeping, we do indeed dare to rejoice.

Meditation: How have you experienced loss and grief? How have they challenged your trust in the gospel promise of life? How have they strengthened your faith in the story's true end?

Prayer: Lord of life, let us know your strength in our losses and rejoice in your promise of life to come.

The Difficult Question

Readings: Ezek 47:1-9, 12; John 5:1-16

Scripture:
   "Do you want to be well?" (John 5:6)

Reflection: Why would Jesus put this question to the sick man by the pool? The poor fellow had lain there for thirty-eight years, trying in vain to beat others to the water when it was stirred up. The locals believed the first one there would be healed—but only the first one. Odds were against this man because he was all alone, without family or friends to help him get there.

   Jesus' question is real in any long-term illness. The sufferer may gradually settle in and begin to call the sickbed home. Hopes of recovery slowly become daydreams, happily entertained but not actually pursued. Familiarity breeds resignation rather than hope.

   The question becomes crucial during Lent. Bible and church use images of sickness to describe the state of sinfulness because both distort the people God wants us to become. Like the long-term patient, we can subtly settle into the assumption that we will never actually be free of those sins we confess again and again, so we give up trying. But, unlike us, God never gives up the struggle to get us up out of that sickbed to live a spiritually healthy life in Christ.

So, in Lent, Jesus shows up again at the soul's sickbed and asks, "Do you want to be well?" If so, the Lenten readings prescribe the treatment: pray, fast, give alms, and treat other people as God's beloved children. Then, once your focus has become broader than yourself, do look at your problem behaviors and seek help in changing them—because, of course, like the sick man in today's story, we cannot get there alone, without any help. The helps are many: God's grace poured out on us through prayer, the sacraments, spiritual reading, good counsel from spiritual directors or wise friends, unexpected inspirations from odd places, like someone's casual remark. But then we have to choose to act on the help given. As Jesus says to the sick man and to us, "Rise, take up your mat, and walk"!

Meditation: Take a look at sins you customarily confess, or commit so regularly that you're ashamed to confess them. Ask for the grace to recognize the opportunities God is giving you this Lent to take the first steps away from them. Oh, and do what God tells you!

Prayer: Healing Lord, grant us the faith, hope, and love to accept responsibility for leaving habitual sins behind with the help of your grace.

Difficult Fact, Difficult Gift

Readings: Isa 49:8-15; John 5:17-30

Scripture:
Sing out, O heavens, and rejoice, O earth,
   break forth into song, you mountains.
For the LORD comforts his people
   and shows mercy to his afflicted. (Isa 49:13)

Reflection: Sunday's joy bubbles over again in today's prophetic first reading, but Jesus' enemies throw a heavy wet blanket over it. They know the prophets. They have seen Jesus comforting and showing mercy to the afflicted of all kinds. They have heard him promise the dawning reign of God. And they are determined to kill him.

Jesus has angered them by breaking the Sabbath and calling God his own Father, though he points out that all his works are God's. And he promises them, in the midst of life's travails, that all stories will come to a happy ending when "the dead will hear the voice of the Son of God, / and those who hear will live." We recall that when we pray "he descended into hell," hell is traditionally understood as the place where the dead awaited him.

To seize that good news, Jesus' hearers—and we among them—have to cope with a difficult fact. What we see as reality is not all there is. Jesus constantly confronts us with the greater reality of God present and working in ways we cannot always see or understand. No matter how carefully and thoroughly we think we have defined God, as Jesus' opponents thought they had, God escapes and becomes once again the uncontrollable "more."

So Jesus' hearers, and we, are confronted with the difficult gift of faith, that relationship with God that opens the road down which Christ comes to save us. The gift comes without tangible guarantees. Hope, yes. Hints, yes. Touches of grace, yes. But no provable facts or definitions because "the more" transcends them.

Jesus' opponents could not accept. They would walk to the edge of the religious facts they trusted, but they would walk no farther, even though Jesus was right there holding out a hand, with crowds of healed sufferers behind him. The gift of faith was just too difficult for them and, in their world, too dangerous, as Jesus' death would prove.

And for us?

Meditation: How do Jesus' promises challenge the way you see reality? How does he ask you to stretch?

Prayer: Lord Jesus Christ, author of life, give us the gift of a faith willing to venture beyond the bounds of common logic and everyday experience into the "more" of God's love.

March 30: Thursday of the Fourth Week of Lent

Accept No Substitutes

Readings: Exod 32:7-14; John 5:31-47

Scripture:
"[My people] have soon turned aside from the way I
    pointed out to them,
   making for themselves a molten calf and worshiping it,
   sacrificing to it and crying out,
   'This is your God, O Israel,
   who brought you out of the land of Egypt!'" (Exod 32:8)

Reflection: Our Lenten road is mapped out in Israel's journey through the desert from Egypt to the Promised Land. On the First Sunday of Lent, we followed Jesus himself into the desert to confront the same Tempter who worked hard during Israel's travels to coax them away from God, their Deliverer. Today's first reading reports one of the Tempter's great successes.

The shorthand version of the story of the golden calf usually accuses Israel of worshiping a false god, but that's not quite what happened. Having apparently lost Moses as the one who took their pleas, complaints, and needs to God on their behalf, they decided to make themselves a substitute. The golden statue of a young bull represented not an alien god but the God whose incredible strength had defeated the great pharaoh and delivered them from Egypt.

We ought not to mock too quickly. Think about the lengths we go to in order to see a conversation partner. Before Skype, all we could do was prop a photo up next to the phone. Israel's former longtime neighbors, the Egyptians, had neither Skype nor photos, so they made statues of their gods to have a visible focus for prayer. So Israel followed their example.

The question for us is this: As we travel our own desert road, what do we do when intermediaries fail and God suddenly disappears or seems to? The Bible, the sacraments, the spiritual books, the good preachers all seem suddenly mute, unable to speak God's word to us in language we can hear. The great saints warn us that this moment must come. Stay with God, they urge us, even if God appears not to have stayed with you.

But it's tempting to create instead mental images of the God we once experienced and to pray before them now to the God of then. Jesus laments in today's gospel, "But you do not want to come to me [as I am for you now] to have life."

Meditation: Have you had moments when God seems suddenly silent, distant, absent? How did you respond? What did you learn?

Prayer: O God of darkness and of light, keep us faithful to you even when we don't experience your presence.

Beware! Holiness on the Loose!

Readings: Wis 2:1a, 12-22; John 7:1-2, 10, 25-30

Scripture:
"[The just one] sets himself against our doings, . . .
To us he is the censure of our thoughts;
    merely to see him is a hardship for us,
Because his life is not like that of others,
    and different are his ways." (Wis 2:12-15)

Reflection: The book of Wisdom was written not long before Christ. As Wisdom literature, its concern is to teach readers how to live rightly, particularly in times of persecution and suffering. Today's first reading offers the example of a hero faithful in every way to God but warns that such a one will stir up the jealous wrath of opponents who read the holy example as a reproach to their own thinking and acting. The passage foretells with uncanny accuracy the conflict between Jesus and the adversaries moving closer and closer to seeking his death as a solution to their growing discomfort.

We sometimes experience the same discomfort around someone who seems genuinely holy. Saints in books or pictures are relatively safe company, but saints loose in the world endanger complacent compromises, part-time faith, and clever excuses for a religion largely unpracticed. The problem is that they contradict our comfortable assumption that, really, no one could actually be expected to *live* gospel. The trouble is that these holy people do. And they come in all shapes and sizes, some of them in circumstances very like our own.

We can take comfort in the fact that we don't actually try to put them to death. But we do sometimes try to suffocate their message. We might make fun of them: "Look at that one! How naive! How old-fashioned! How boring!" How *anything* except relevant to us who also claim to be believers. Or we might stay out of their way and keep them out of ours. Or we might just ignore them and change the channel, as it were, to people less threatening to our consciences.

Probably not a good idea, say today's readings, because we're really making fun of, avoiding, or turning off Christ. That's the thing about genuinely holy people—they actually are Christ loose in the world.

Meditation: Are there genuinely good believers who make you uncomfortable? Why? How do you respond to them?

Prayer: Word of God made flesh, teach us to hear your voice in the witness of good Christians around us and to look honestly at the witness we ourselves give.

Difference or Division?

Readings: Jer 11:18-20; John 7:40-53

Scripture:
So a division occurred in the crowd because of him. . . .
Then each went to his own house. (John 7:43, 53)

Reflection: Jesus certainly stirred up differences of opinion. When asked who people thought he was, his disciples reported all sorts of views (Matt 6:14). Late in his ministry, John's gospel reports that the differences have continued and intensified. Some think he's "the Prophet," the one predicted by Moses. Some think he's "the Christ" but others argue against a Messiah from Galilee. Their differences grow heated, but they can come to no agreement. So they all pack up and go home separately.

Down through the centuries since, Christians have often been divided in our interpretations and opinions of Christ. Historically, believers have again and again latched onto one or other aspect of the Christ-mystery and divided into opposing camps, each waving its flag against the others at least verbally. Sometimes, alas, such differences have bred violence.

Conviction is important, but Christian conviction lives within a framework defined by the great commandments of love for God and neighbor—and we are all more than neighbors in the unity of the one Body of Christ. Unity is not totalitarian mind control. Nor is it a feeling of neighborliness amid anarchy of thought. Rather, it has a responsibility to three principles: first, respect for the unique inspirations and gifts of particular individuals and schools of belief; second, recognition that every set of inspirations and gifts has limitations to be owned humbly by those who hold them; and third, acceptance of the overriding reality of the Body as the one Christ embracing all this messy humanity in our very messiness and transforming us into a communion of faith in mutual honor and love.

Apart from the larger concerns of reconciling ecumenical and interfaith differences, perhaps we as believing individuals could draw closer to living this responsibility if, unlike the parties in today's gospel, we did not each go home to our own homes and slam the door behind us, grumbling all the while about "those others" outside. Perhaps we could instead open the doors and invite others in for a conversation in quest of mutual understanding and respect.

Meditation: Think of members of your parish or prayer group with whom you disagree radically on some aspect of Jesus or other. What could you do to understand them better?

Prayer: Father, expand our hearts to appreciate those with whom we disagree so that, by the light of your all-inclusive love, we may all become united in mutual respect even when we cannot agree with one another's views.

Coming Out, Going In

Readings: Ezek 37:12-14; Rom 8:8-11; John 11:1-45 or John 11:3-7, 17, 20-27, 33b-45

Scripture:
   "Lazarus, come out!" (John 11:43)

Reflection: Picture it. A cave sealed with a stone, a crowd gathered—the knot of neighbors come to offer sympathy, the two sisters, the disciples—and Jesus standing facing the tomb. Someone rolls back the stone, over Martha's protest at the stench. Jesus prays to his Father that those gathered may believe. The tension rises. Jesus cries out loudly, "Lazarus, come out!" The tension becomes unbearable. Then, from the mouth of the tomb hops the figure of a man tied hand and foot, wrapped up like a mummy, face covered, able to see nothing. Imagine the gasp—and perhaps the front row shrinking back in horror at the sight. Finally, Jesus calls for someone to untie him and strip off the shroud. Then the curtain falls on spectators murmuring new belief in this man who raises the dead. Unforgettable, this tense drama culminating in the unbelievable suddenly believed.

   One wonders a bit if Lazarus was the only one raised from the dead that day. The last sentence has all the drama of what went before, but it's quieter: "Now many . . . who had come

. . . and seen what he had done began to believe in him."
Unbelief is its own kind of thick shroud.

Two weeks before Easter Sunday, we spot the preview for
what it is. There will be another tomb sealed with a stone,
shut up for three days, and then empty of all but the burial
clothes and the face covering. But no one will be there to
witness the dead one rising.

There is another difference, a greater one. In Lazarus's
story, Jesus stands outside the tomb and summons Lazarus
to come out. In his own story, Jesus himself goes into the
tomb to bring out with him all the dead confined there. In
our stories, when we find ourselves in the cold dark, bound
by unbelief or fear or hatred or whatever else has deadened
us in spirit, Jesus stands at the entrance to our tomb and calls
us to come out. Then he comes in and gets us. More, in the
imagery of the prophets (e.g., Isa 40:11), he carries us out
because we are too weak to walk out on our own.

Meditation: Are there places in your inner being that feel
dead? What is confining you there? Ask Jesus to come in, all
the way in to where you are trapped, and get you. He will.

Prayer: Jesus, risen Lord of Life, deliver us!

The Greatest Mercy

Readings: Dan 13:1-9, 15-17, 19-30, 33-62 or Dan 13:41c-62;
John 8:1-11

Scripture:
"Let the one among you who is without sin
be the first to throw a stone at her." (John 8:7)

Reflection: Jesus' opponents never seem to learn. Here they are again, trying to trap him in the kind of legal snare he always walks out of. Their first mistake is to shame the woman, dragging her onto center stage and shining a spotlight on her sin. Even worse, they have no real interest in her. She is merely cannon fodder in their relentless attack on Jesus, the excuse for trotting out their big gun: the law of Moses. "Look," they say, "here is a woman caught committing adultery. The law says to stone her to death. What do you say?" They stand back, brushes dripping, to admire the corner into which they think they have painted him: legal observance versus the mercy toward sinners he's known for. Whichever he chooses, he loses. Then they have him!

Jesus remains as slippery as ever. He seems to ignore them, busy scribbling on the ground. They badger him until he rises to confront them. He doesn't focus on the woman at all, or on the law. He focuses on them. He offers a third choice: let whoever has never broken the law you are so fiercely protecting here throw the first stone.

At least they are honest. They drop their stones and slink away.

Only then does Jesus turn to the woman. He does not whitewash her sin. He asks no questions about extenuating circumstances. He offers no criticism of the law he has forced his adversaries to set aside. He wouldn't.

From the beginning of the human story, God has stuck by the inexorable principle of adult morality: choose the action, choose the consequences. When people turn and beg forgiveness, God does not withdraw the law broken but commutes the sentence to a change of behavior as Jesus does here—though in this case, the woman herself makes no excuse and asks for no unmerited pardon. Perhaps her obvious misery says enough.

Jesus grants the accusers and the accused, both guilty but honest, the greatest mercy: the chance to change.

Meditation: How do you respond to others' sins? Do you ever focus on them to keep from focusing on your own? Do you fear God's condemnation if you admit your sins?

Prayer: Jesus, mercy of God, make us honest about our own sins and compassionate toward other sinners, so that we may truly reflect your love.

April 4: Tuesday of the Fifth Week of Lent

Lifted Up

Readings: Num 21:4-9; John 8:21-30

Scripture:
   "When you lift up the Son of Man,
   then you will realize that I AM . . . " (John 8:28)

Reflection: We read these two passages, the story of the serpent lifted up on a pole by Moses in the desert and Jesus' odd reference to being lifted up, with insider knowledge: we have seen and will see again on Good Friday the unforgettable image of Jesus Christ, Son of God made Son of Man, nailed to a cross of wood and lifted up for all to see on Mount Calvary and in our churches.

In the desert, the Israelites engage in one of their countless gripe sessions against the wretched provisions God has provided for them on their journey, provisions that have saved their lives. This time God responds by sending poisonous serpents among the people, many of whom are bitten and die. The people repent of their complaints and beg to have the serpents removed. Moses, at God's command, makes a bronze image of the serpent and holds it up on a pole so that whoever sees it is healed and does not die. Thus the people are saved by the very image of what was causing their death.

The crucifix we reverence on Good Friday does the same. On it, we see our own humanity, in our case always subject to the sinful selfishness that first led to our mortality, but in Jesus' case free of sin. He has taken on the mortality that was the first consequence of sin, but he has replaced the selfishness with a love we can hardly imagine. On the cross, we see and are saved by the image of what caused our death—our humanity—transformed into the cause of our salvation. The Word of God took on our humanity, fallen and disfigured though it was, and transmuted it from within into the source of our redemption by the power of his love.

When he is lifted up on the cross before our eyes, we see the depths of love of God made visible, and we acclaim him as our Savior.

Meditation: Spend some time before a crucifix. Reflect on the strength of Jesus' love for you and for all of us. How does that affect you?

Prayer: Christ Jesus, crucified for love of all people and risen to give us new life, deliver us from the death of sin and raise us up in love.

But If Not

Readings: Dan 3:14-20, 91-92, 95; John 8:31-42

Scripture:
"If our God, whom we serve,
   can save us from the white-hot furnace
   and from your hands, O king, may he save us!
But even if he will not, know, O king,
   that we will not serve your god . . . " (Dan 3:17-18)

Reflection: One of the most moving stories from World War II is the deliverance of thousands of allied troops trapped on the beach at Dunkirk in France. With the sea at their back and German troops advancing toward them, the British signal officer sent a three-word message to the British command in London: "But if not." British command recognized the words spoken by the three young men threatened with Nebuchadnezzar's fiery furnace if they refused to bow down to his god. They did not give in. Neither would the allied soldiers. If they could not be saved, they would stay faithful to the death. In response, the British navy and hundreds of private boat owners crossed the channel and snatched the beleaguered troops out of enemy hands.

Jesus is in something of a Dunkirk position in today's gospel. His enemies are closing in. If only he would abandon this blasphemous claim that God is his father! But Jesus will not give in, though he knows he will not be delivered from death when the time for it comes. Instead, he will be raised up again.

Fidelity in the face of threat always stirs us. We hear stories of children cut down before their parents' eyes because neither will deny Christ. We read accounts of aid workers choosing probable death from violence or disease rather than abandoning those they came to help. We hear, in other words, stories of our own best selves, or the best selves we would like to be when forced to choose between faithfulness and harm. And these are the selves we are made and called to be in Christ, who remained faithful to truth and love even in the teeth of death. Our circumstances may be less dramatic, but fidelity that stands firm in the face of adversity is worthy of the name "Christian" nonetheless.

Meditation: When have you felt threatened in small or great ways for your fidelity to Christ? Remember the grace you were given then and call on it now, because fidelity does not belong to us alone but even more to our God.

Prayer: O faithful Christ, make us staunch in fidelity to you in all the circumstances of our lives.

Now Is Forever

Readings: Gen 17:3-9; John 8:51-59

Scripture:
"I will maintain my covenant with you
   and your descendants after you
   throughout the ages as an everlasting pact,
   to be your God and the God of your descendants after
      you." (Gen 17:7)

Reflection: In today's gospel, Jesus' opponents are understandably confused by his timeline. Jesus claims to have existed before Abraham. How could that be, given the centuries elapsed between the ancient patriarch and the thirty-something rabbi? But Jesus is making the connection with Abraham on the basis not of chronology but of promise and fulfillment, something his hearers are not yet prepared to grasp. In hindsight the connection is easier for us to see.

In the first reading, God makes the great promise to Abraham: "I will make nations of you . . . / I will maintain my covenant with you / throughout the ages as an everlasting pact." The covenant, in other words, will outlive the ordinary limits of time because both God and Abraham's heirs will also outlive them. Unimaginable to Jesus' hearers!

It might still sound like wishful nonsense were it not for Jesus, who entered time from eternity and returned from time to eternity through his death and resurrection. But he did not leave the denizens of time behind and abandoned. Jesus is the covenant in the flesh, the One in whom God and humanity are irrevocably bound together in a way neither Abraham nor Jesus' interlocutors could possibly have foreseen. As long as the risen Christ lives—which will be forever—the covenant continues. It is like an unbreakably woven steel hawser running through the years from first to last, from Alpha to Omega—and Omega has no end. And where Christ, the living covenant, endures, so will we who are baptized into him.

But don't look so far down the road that you lose sight of the present. Forever begins again for us right now, this Lent, as we prepare to take on or recommit ourselves to the life into which Christ has raised us.

Meditation: Take a closer look at your life as you are living it right now. What aspects of it, what habits of being, what relationships do you hope to carry with you into eternity? What decisions does that mean for the present?

Prayer: Eternal and ever-living God, gather us gently toward our future with you in Christ by guiding our Lenten conversion today.

Deliverance?

Readings: Jer 20:10-13; John 10:31-42

Scripture:
Then they tried again to arrest him;
  but he escaped from their power. (John 10:39)

Reflection: In the first reading, the beleaguered prophet Jeremiah, confronted on every side by hostile enemies intent on his destruction, much as Jesus is in the gospel, exclaims in faith, "But the Lord is with me, like a mighty champion: / my persecutors will stumble, they will not triumph. . . . / For he has rescued the life of the poor / from the power of the wicked!" Jesus can make the same claim with even greater authority, for he knows "that the Father is in me and I am in the Father." Yet neither Jeremiah nor Jesus will enjoy the kind of happy ending they look forward to, or so it seems.

Jeremiah's enemies cast him into a dry cistern to starve to death, but he is rescued to live out his life in exile in Egypt. Jesus' enemies, of course, succeed in having him put to death on a cross. One might accuse both of them, as nonbelievers do, of naive optimism in their faith that God will deliver them.

The irony is that God will, but not by sparing them from death. All sufferers reprieved from hostile foes or illness or the ravages of age do, in the end, die. Even God will not save them from death, however great their faith and fervent their prayer. And Jesus does not ask, except perhaps in that one moment in the garden when he begs the Father to take the cup away (Luke 22:42). The secret, known to people of faith but never understood by those who cannot believe, is that God delivers Jesus, and with him all of us, not *from* death but *through* death, beyond which there are no further threats. By that deliverance, all Jesus' enemies are indeed defeated, most especially the great enemy behind all the others, the power of evil.

In Christ, then, every prayer for deliverance is ultimately answered even when enemies seem invincible and suffering unending. Christian prayer is always justified in its trust and praise.

Meditation: Who are your enemies? They may not be people but circumstances, habits, or something else. Present them to Christ on the cross. Imagine his love transforming them into opportunities rather than destroyers.

Prayer: O God of power, deliver us and those we love from every hostile force through the power of Christ's death and resurrection.

Promises Kept

Readings: Ezek 37:21-28; John 11:45-56

Scripture:
"[It] is better for you
that one man should die instead of the people,
so that the whole nation may not perish." (John 11:50)

Reflection: Caiaphas, high priest in Jerusalem during Jesus' last days, has gone down in Christian history for this double-edged prognostication. The actual context was a Sanhedrin worried that if Jesus kept gathering followers, the Romans would take control to prevent an uprising, as Rome was known to do. Caiaphas proposes to remove the danger with a trade: Jesus' death for the survival of the people. Ironically, that is God's own plan: that Jesus die "not only for the nation, / but also to gather into one the dispersed children of God" (John 11:52), as God promised centuries before through the prophet Ezekiel (Ezek 37:21-22).

Scripture assures us again and again that God's promises are always kept, but rarely in the ways we anticipate. Think of Abraham and Sarah; think of David the shepherd boy; think of the people sunk in the gloom of exile in Babylon. They would never have imagined how God's promises to them would play out. Ezekiel never dreamed that the new shepherd-prince David he prophesied in the first reading would die to gather up God's scattered children. Caiaphas never imagined how Jesus' death would in fact deliver God's people from annihilation.

Our own vision of the future is never more than partial. Even as we continue at every Mass to proclaim our faith in the saving power of Jesus present in the Eucharist, we are surprised by the deaths of martyrs, the failures of the church's political dominions, and the earthquakes caused by scandal. Yet the Good News continues to thrive. God works with unexpected tools through unexpected situations to keep the great promise: "I will make with them a covenant of peace; / it shall be an everlasting covenant with them, / and I will multiply them, and put my sanctuary among them forever" (Ezek 37:26-27). At Easter we will celebrate the fact that God's work always ends in ultimate success no enemy can really foil.

Meditation: Think of times in your life when the future has seemed to promise only unremitting bleakness. Did you catch glimpses of the triumph of light over that darkness? Did others help restore your hope? Have you in turn done that for others amid all the bad news we read and see daily?

Prayer: Lord of life and hope, open our eyes to your power at work unexpectedly even through the darkest of circumstances.

Crowds

Readings: Matt 21:1-11 (Procession with the Palms); Isa 50:4-7; Phil 2:6-11; Matt 26:14–27:66 or Matt 27:11-54

Scripture:
The crowds preceding him and those following
   kept crying out and saying:
     "Hosanna to the Son of David . . . " (Matt 21:9)

Reflection: Wherever there's a motorcade, there's bound to be a horde of people crowding the sidewalks in hope of catching sight of the celebrity in the main car, be it movie star, president, or pope. Crowds have always loved a spectacle. Best of all, they love a spectacle that gives them some kind of access, however brief and distant, to someone important. The people of Jerusalem in Jesus' day were no different.

First came the procession of the enigmatic figure who might be a prophet, or the king long prophesied (cf. Zech 9:9), or even the Messiah, depending on which whispers you believed. Everyone, it seems, rushed to get a look. "Who is this?" the city asked. Not a horse-mounted Roman soldier, nor a slave-borne aristocrat, nor an exotic visitor from the East, but simply "Jesus the prophet, from Nazareth in Galilee," riding on a donkey colt. I wonder how many of them went away disappointed that there were no miracles, no shows of power, no spectacle at all, really, except the strange parade.

Later came another kind of spectacle: a bedraggled, bleeding figure dragging a wooden beam through the streets up to Calvary. Crowds seem to have gathered along the road then too. Were there whispers about a prophet, a king, a Messiah? Or about the healer who had worked such wonders? Surely.

Some of these crowds followed Jesus up the hill for the grisly spectacle of crucifixion. No palms and hosannas then, just the mockery of onlookers (Matt 27:38b-41) and the indifferent cruelty of Roman soldiers going about their grisly business.

We look at crowds gathered for a spectacle and see only a sea of faces. We can be sure that Jesus saw the persons shouting "Hosanna!" and standing by the road as he struggled toward Calvary, hanging about within sight of the cross, each one unique. "Love your neighbor," he said, not "your neighbors." You can love a person. You cannot love a crowd. And it was for every human person he died, not for the faceless masses.

Meditation: The next time you see a crowd event, look at the faces. Try to see them as Jesus sees them, with the eyes of love.

Prayer: Jesus, you see the people in every crowd. Grant that we may look beyond the anonymity of the throng and see individuals you love.

The Heart of Discipleship

Readings: Isa 42:1-7; John 12:1-11

Scripture:
Mary took a liter of costly perfumed oil . . .
   and anointed the feet of Jesus and dried them with her
      hair . . . (John 12:3)

Reflection: Mary of Bethany—Martha and Lazarus's sister, Jesus' friend and disciple—reappears in today's gospel. In Luke's gospel, written earlier than John's, she provoked her sister's ire by choosing to sit at Jesus' feet like a disciple and listen to him rather than helping with the meal. Now she again flouts convention by anointing Jesus' feet with expensive perfumed oil and drying them with her hair. Again she provokes ire, this time from Judas. Ironically, he protests her disregard for Jesus' teaching about the poor, though he, not she, will prove to be the false disciple. In neither story does Mary utter a word of self-defense, but Jesus defends her in startling terms—in Luke, for choosing the one essential, a listening discipleship; here for expressing her discipleship in an act Jesus deems prophetic.

   In both cases, Mary goes to the heart of discipleship: the mystery of Jesus himself, in Luke as the Word of God speaking in their midst, now in John as the Anointed One who will die. She annoys her sister Martha by ignoring the precept of hospitality to a guest. She angers Judas by ignoring the poor. Jesus says once again that Mary, disciple to the core, has her priorities right: the person of this Messiah outweighs even his own ethical teaching. There are times, and this is one of them, when the disciple must let Jesus' teachings fade into the background to focus attention entirely on him and own fully who he really is. And, as Jesus himself will, Mary sets aside all concern for her own good name to do what discipleship bids her because she above all of them has truly understood the Truth he will claim at the Last Supper to be (John 14:6).

We live in a doing world, busy about works of all sorts. As disciples, we do our best to carry out the works of the gospel. But Mary teaches us the core of discipleship: knowing Jesus, the source and definition of all good works.

Meditation: What has your focus been this Lent? How has your Lenten penance brought you to know Christ more deeply?

Prayer: Lord and Savior Jesus Christ, grant us the grace to recognize you as the source and center of our life as disciples.

April 11: Tuesday of Holy Week

Chosen

Readings: Isa 49:1-6; John 13:21-33, 36-38

Scripture:
The LORD called me from birth, . . .
You are my servant, he said to me,
   Israel, through whom I show my glory. (Isa 49:1, 3)

Reflection: So accustomed have we become to casting Judas as the ultimate betrayer for selling Jesus out to his enemies that we can overlook the real extent of his betrayal. We know very little about Judas. What we do know comes to us largely from the pen of a biased evangelist who exposes him as a miser and a thief before he ever becomes a traitor. In John's portrait, Judas is painted in dark colors, with no hint of light, but for balance, we should remember that, whatever his character defects, Judas was born one of God's chosen people, called by God from birth like all of us, and appointed Jesus' disciple.

So in handing Jesus over to his enemies, Judas betrayed not only his Master but also his heritage, his history, and his vocation. His tragedy is not limited to the last act of his personal drama: betrayal and suicide. His tragedy includes the longer story of a person twisted and lost, one who came into the world beloved by his Creator and destined for good but threw it all away.

We don't know the details of that story, but we can heed its warning. We also came into the world beloved by our Creator, chosen and gifted for good we grow into. Along the way, we have our own choices to make, some small, some momentous: Will I choose friends wisely, will I learn, will I take the path God lays out for me, will I do good or ill? And never mind the drama: "good" is not always throwing myself in front of a truck to save a child, and "ill" is not always grabbing for the thirty pieces of silver. Good and ill come in all sizes and shapes, most of them not worthy of mention in the evening news, but all of them vital to the shape our story and our world will take and the ending it will come to.

Meditation: Think back about your life's crossroads moments. When and why did you choose for "good," and when for "ill"? How have those choices shaped your life? What choices is God offering you now?

Prayer: O God, Creator and Redeemer, guide us through the crossroads small and great, so that we may truly grow into your faithful servants.

April 12: Wednesday of Holy Week

Betrayers

Readings: Isa 50:4-9a; Matt 26:14-25

Scripture:
"It would be better for that man if he had never been
  born." (Matt 26:24)

Reflection: In the passion story, Judas and Peter have betrayal in common. Judas betrays Jesus to those who seek to
kill him, apparently for no better reason than a handful of
coins. Peter betrays himself on the eve of the crucifixion
when he denies being Jesus' follower, apparently for his own
safety (John 18:17). Peter will repent (Matt 27:3-4) and accept
Jesus' forgiveness. Judas will repent but he will accept no
forgiveness, not even his own. Instead, he will hang himself
(Matt 27:5). It is easy to say of him, as Jesus did, "better for
that man if he had never been born."

Judas remains forever a mystery. However he began, he
ended up a man of contradictions, chosen by Christ, reviled
as a thief by John, despised by the authorities who paid for
his information, and utterly despairing of himself. We don't
know why Judas's life took the turns that led him to this end.
But we do know his greatest mistake.

During his years as a disciple he missed the most important thing about the Master he had agreed to follow. He may
have learned all the right words, but he never learned to

know the Person who spoke them. Jesus expressed frustration with hypocrisy and blindness. He even uttered dramatic woes against the towns that refused to accept him and his message (e.g., Matt 11:20-24). But he never refused compassion to a repentant sinner. Never. And somehow Judas missed it.

Lent offers us an extended time in which to seek what St. Paul calls "the supreme good" of knowing Christ more deeply, more intimately, more truly (see Phil 3:8-9) Whatever we may have done in the way of fasting, prayer, almsgiving, and other good works, the underlying purpose has been to free us of the claustrophobic self so we can plunge into deeper communion with the One who is God's mercy.

Missed it? Don't worry. Lent, like every other liturgical season, is a rehearsal for all of life. And the invitation to know and love and live in Christ remains open all year round.

Meditation: How have you come to know Jesus better this Lent? How do you feel called to grow toward knowing and loving him even more deeply in the months to come?

Prayer: Lord Jesus Christ, grant that daily we may see you more clearly, love you more dearly, and follow you more nearly.

April 13: Holy Thursday (Maundy Thursday)

Bread for the Journey

Readings: Exod 12:1-8, 11-14; 1 Cor 11:23-26; John 13:1-15

Scripture:
[Jesus] took bread, and . . . said, "This is my body that is
for you." (1 Cor 11:23-24)

Reflection: Tonight we hear the story of the first Passover
meal eaten by the Hebrew slaves in Egypt on the vigil of
their journey to freedom in the Promised Land (Exod 12).
They ate unleavened bread, quickly made and easily carried.
According to the first three gospels, Jesus and his disciples
shared that other Passover meal we remember tonight. There
Jesus held out unleavened bread and said something very
odd: "This is my body that is for you."

Jesus was preparing for his own Passover. When early
Christians struggled to comprehend the impossible mystery
of a slain Messiah, they borrowed the familiar language of
Passover to make some kind of sense of Jesus' death. Jesus
was slain on the vigil of Passover, at the hour when the paschal lambs were sacrificed (John 19:14). John the Baptist had
said of him, "Behold, the Lamb of God" (John 1:29). On Calvary, he would complete the journey from the world en-
slaved by sin to the land of everlasting freedom. And he
called us to follow.

But it would be a longer, harder journey than Israel's, and far more demanding. Jesus had already sketched out bits of the map. His followers would meet a gate too narrow for excess baggage (Matt 7:13; 19:24), abandon the familiar and the comfortable (Matt 19:27-29), meet persecution (e.g., John 15:21), and face death (John 16:2). Jesus knew it would be hard. He knew disciples would grow weary and dream seductive dreams of the Egypt left behind (cf. Exod 16:13). So he left us food for the journey: "This is my Body, take and eat."

As we follow him, we might wonder what food *he* had on *his* paschal journey? He himself said, "My food is to do the will of the one who sent me" (John 4:34). This offers a clue to the Bread he gives us. In becoming part of our bodies, this holy Bread transforms us into his Body. His journey becomes ours. Thus we assume his life of intense obedience to the single law of love for God and neighbor that he dramatizes in the washing of feet and lives out on the cross.

Eat up. We have a long way to go—a lifetime, in fact.

Meditation: Good food strengthens. How has the Eucharist strengthened you?

Prayer: Bread of Life, nourish us with your love so that we may live it faithfully on our way.

April 14: Good Friday of the Lord's Passion

The Gate to Glory

Readings: Isa 52:13–53:12; Heb 4:14-16; 5:7-9; John 18:1–19:42

Scripture:
[Jesus] said,
   "It is finished."
And bowing his head, he handed over the spirit.
   (John 19:30)

Reflection: On the First Sunday of Lent, we read the story of the original human couple in Eden but left them before their tragic exodus from the protected garden to the harsh world beyond when the gate closed behind them and a fierce guard was posted to prevent return (see Gen 3). But that fiery sword-bearer has never stopped humanity from dreaming of our lost utopia and trying to find our way back.

However, the hard fact is that we must travel forward, not backward, on life's road. And the road ends at the garden wall humanity could never breach or climb, no matter how hard people tried. The wall is death. For millennia, no traveler could find a ladder or a gate, despite growing belief in life on the other side. But when Jesus died, he at last burst open a gate in the wall and left it open behind him for all who would follow.

It is a difficult gate. Narrow, Jesus suggested (Matt 7:13). Cross-shaped, says St. John of the Cross. As we get close we see that the rough wooden frame is still marked by the blood of the Paschal Lamb who first passed through.

The gate has two sides. Our side is darkness as we read last Sunday in Matthew 27:45, when darkness covered the whole earth as Jesus hung dying. The darkness frightens us because it's all we can see from here. But the far side of the gate is bathed in light, the light from which Jesus came (cf. John 1:9) and to which he returns. In John's gospel, he knows the light is there. At the Last Supper, he asks the Father to glorify him (John 17:5). In the context of the Old Testament imagery John often relies on, Jesus is praying to return to the glory he once left behind (cf. Phil 2:6-7). In John's gospel, then, the cross is not a tragedy but the gate to glory.

Meditation: Have you ever been at or heard about the death-bed of someone who caught a glimpse through the gate to the light? How did it affect those present?

Prayer: Lord Jesus, you are the gate of life. Draw us by faith and prayer through the cross to the garden of light awaiting us.

April 15: Holy Saturday and Easter Vigil

Emptiness Filled

Readings: Gen 1:1–2:2; Gen 22:1-18; Exod 14:15–15:1; Isa
54:5-14; Isa 55:1-11; Bar 3:9-15, 32–4:4; Ezek 36:16-17a, 18-28;
Rom 6:3-11; Matt 28:1-10

Scripture:
"Do not be afraid!
I know that you are seeking Jesus the crucified.
He is not here, for he has been raised . . . " (Matt 28:6)

Reflection: "[T]here is a great silence on earth today, a great
silence and stillness," said an ancient preacher on Holy Saturday. Silence, stillness, emptiness—an empty sanctuary, an
empty tabernacle, an empty cross. The early church even
maintained the Good Friday fast through Holy Saturday, as
some do today.

It is tempting to fill the emptiness with activity—doing
the Saturday shopping, cleaning the house for tomorrow,
filling the church with flowers. But then we lose the day's
gift. "Prayer begins at the edge of emptiness," said Abraham
Joshua Heschel. Today's silence recalls the first disciples'
experience of the whole world lying empty because the Lord
was gone. That emptiness calls us to prayer. Prayer at the
edge of emptiness offers no consolation because God seems
absent. It is our cry of faith into the abyss precisely because
we believe against all evidence that God lives, is with us,

hears our every whisper. For many people today, faced with the evil breaking over the world in waves of unstoppable violence, prayer at the edge of emptiness is the only prayer there is. Even if this is not our own experience, today is the day to go and stand beside them in spirit and lend them our strength as we borrow theirs.

We can because we know that at the far side of the Holy Saturday emptiness lies one even greater: the emptiness of the tomb that held the Savior yesterday. We will gather this evening on that far side of emptiness and fill the air with the fragrance of incense, the ringing of bells, the singing of alleluias. The irrevocable emptiness of the tomb is God's assertion that every other emptiness is an illusion filled with a Presence we cannot see. "I am with you always," said Jesus to his disciples after Easter (Matt 28:20). As we listen to all the other words read and sung tonight, we watch the light spread through our churches from a single flame, we receive the living Bread—and we know the promise is true.

Alleluia!

Meditation: Spend time today before an empty cross. When evening comes, set a light before it, and give thanks.

Prayer: Lord Jesus, come to us in our emptiness and fill us with your loving presence.

Song for the Journey

Readings: Acts 10:34a, 37-43; Col 3:1-4 or 1 Cor 5:6b-8; John 20:1-9 or Matt 28:1-10

Scripture:
For you have died, and your life is hidden with Christ in
    God.
When Christ your life appears,
    then you too will appear with him in glory. (Col 3:3-4)

Reflection: Alleluia! Today and throughout the Easter season to come, that's our song. In Gregorian chant, gospel style, and glorious polyphony, alleluia washes through our churches, chasing away the struggles of Lent, the pain of the Passion, the silence of Holy Saturday. Flame replaces darkness, and flowers replace bare sanctuaries.

The hard season is done, the season of celebration has begun. I can't help hearing a friend's annual Easter refrain ringing in my ears: "Alleluia, Lent is over!" She sings it privately, of course.

It isn't true. Amid the Easter alleluias, Lent goes underground, but its work goes on for both those who came to it already baptized and those newly emerged from the baptismal waters. Lent goes on because we have a long journey of conversion yet to make as Sundays again tempt us out to the shopping mall instead of to church, or annoying neighbors still annoy, or bad habits temporarily squelched reemerge when we're not looking. Christ now enthroned in glory urges us forward, but he does not allow us to skip over real life to get to the happy ending we look forward to. Life is still our workshop, discernment and discipline our tools, love our practice and our goal.

But alleluia lightens the way. There is reason for joy right here, right now, it seems to say. Catch glimpses of it over there in that child's laughter, or here in the glory of that sunrise, or this evening when a loved one calls, or anytime light wins against the shadow, as it has and always will (John 1:5). How can that be when the evening news or the morning paper or the gossip at the grocery store so often bears tales of darkness seeming to envelop the world? Christ—crucified, buried, and risen—answers, "I am with you always!" (Matt 28:20).

Even here, in the midst of tribulations and temptations, let us sing alleluia, says St. Augustine. Sing not to escape the work of conversion but to lighten the load. But sing as travelers do, he says, because we have a ways yet to go. Sing alleluia, but keep going!

Meditation: What gifts and challenges will you carry forward from here?

Prayer: Christ our life, be our alleluia and our goal as we travel forward. Grant us the joy of your risen presence and the strength of your love to sustain us on the journey.

References

March 2: Thursday after Ash Wednesday
Walter Ciszek, SJ, *With God in Russia* (New York: The America Press, 1964).

Immaculée Ilibagiza, *Left to Tell: Discovering God Amidst the Rwandan Holocaust* (Carlsbad, CA: Hay House, 2006, 2014).

March 5: First Sunday of Lent
Several early church preachers interpreted Jesus' baptism this way. See, for example, the passage from a sermon of St. Gregory of Nazienzen found in *The Liturgy of the Hours*, Office of Readings, Baptism of the Lord.

March 6: Monday of the First Week of Lent
Austin Flannery, ed., "Chapter V: The Universal Call to Holiness," *Lumen Gentium* (Dogmatic Constitution on the Church) 40, in *Vatican Council II: Constitutions, Decrees, Declarations; The Basic Sixteen Documents* (Collegeville, MN: Liturgical Press, 2014).

March 8: Wednesday of the First Week of Lent
Recommended reading: "Revelation," Flannery O'Connor, *The Complete Stories* (New York: Farrar, Straus and Giroux, 1971).

March 10: Friday of the First Week of Lent
See Pope Francis, *Misericordiae Vultus*: Bull of Indiction of the Extraordinary Jubilee of Mercy, April 11, 2015, https://w2.vatican.va/content/francesco/en/apost_letters/documents/papa-francesco_bolla_20150411_misericordiae-vultus.html.

March 13: Monday of the Second Week of Lent
Dick Francis, *Bolt* (New York: Berkeley Books, 2005), 208.

March 26: Fourth Sunday of Lent
Abraham Joshua Heschel, *God in Search of Man: A Philosophy of Judaism* (New York: Farrar, Straus and Giroux, 1955).

April 11: Tuesday of Holy Week
Prayer adapted from St. Richard of Chichester (1197–1253).

April 14: Good Friday of the Lord's Passion
See John of the Cross, *Spiritual Canticle*, in *The Liturgy of the Hours*, Office of Readings, Second Reading, December 14.

April 15: Holy Saturday and Easter Vigil
Ancient Homily for Holy Saturday, *The Liturgy of the Hours*, Office of Readings, Second Reading, Holy Saturday.

April 16: Easter Sunday: The Resurrection of the Lord
Paraphrase of St. Augustine, sermon, in *The Liturgy of the Hours*, Saturday of the Thirty-Fourth Week in Ordinary Time.